D0566845

POCKET
prayers
for MILITARY LIFE

POCKET
prayers
for MILITARY LIFE

40 SIMPLE PRAYERS THAT BRING
FAITH AND COURAGE

MAX LUCADO
WITH MARK MYNHEIR

THOMAS NELSON
Since 1798

© 2016 Max Lucado

All rights reserved. No portion of this book may be reproduced, stored in a retrieval system, or transmitted in any form or by any means—electronic, mechanical, photocopy, recording, scanning, or other—except for brief quotations in critical reviews or articles, without the prior written permission of the publisher.

Published in Nashville, Tennessee, by Thomas Nelson. Thomas Nelson is a registered trademark of HarperCollins Christian Publishing, Inc.

Thomas Nelson titles may be purchased in bulk for educational, business, fund-raising, or sales promotional use. For information, please e-mail SpecialMarkets@ThomasNelson.com.

Unless otherwise noted, Scripture quotations are taken from the New King James Version®. © 1982 by Thomas Nelson. Used by permission. All rights reserved.

Scripture quotations marked NCV are from the New Century Version®. © 2005 by Thomas Nelson. Used by permission. All rights reserved.

Scripture quotations marked NIV are from the Holy Bible, New International Version®, NIV®. Copyright © 1973, 1978, 1984, 2011 by Biblica, Inc.® Used by permission of Zondervan. All rights reserved worldwide. www.zondervan.com. The "NIV" and "New International Version" are trademarks registered in the United States Patent and Trademark Office by Biblica, Inc.®

Scripture quotations marked NLT are from the Holy Bible, New Living Translation. © 1996, 2004, 2007, 2013 by Tyndale House Foundation. Used by permission of Tyndale House Publishers, Inc., Carol Stream, Illinois 60188. All rights reserved.

Any Internet addresses, phone numbers, or company or product information printed in this book are offered as a resource and are not intended in any way to be or to imply an endorsement by Thomas Nelson, nor does Thomas Nelson vouch for the existence, content, or services of these sites, phone numbers, companies, or products beyond the life of this book.

ISBN 978-0-7180-7832-4 (eBook)

Library of Congress Control Number: 2015956801
ISBN 978-0-7180-7734-1

Printed in China

20 21 22   DSC   10 9 8 7 6 5 4 3 2

The Pocket Prayer

Hello, my name is Max. I'm a recovering prayer wimp. I doze off when I pray. My thoughts zig, then zag, then zig again. Distractions swarm like gnats on a summer night. If attention deficit disorder applies to prayer, I am afflicted. When I pray, I think of a thousand things I need to do. I forget the one thing I set out to do: pray.

Some people excel in prayer. They inhale heaven and exhale God. They are the SEAL Team Six of intercession. They would rather pray than sleep. Why is it that I sleep when I pray? They belong to the PGA: Prayer Giants Association. I am a card-carrying member of the PWA: Prayer Wimps Anonymous.

Can you relate? It's not that we don't pray at all. We all pray some.

On tearstained pillows we pray.

In grand liturgies we pray.

At the sight of geese in flight, we pray.

Quoting ancient devotions, we pray.

We pray to stay sober, centered, or solvent. We pray when the lump is deemed malignant. When the money runs out before the month does. When the unborn baby hasn't kicked in a while. We all pray . . . some.

But wouldn't we all like to pray . . .

More?

Better?

Deeper?

Stronger?

With more fire, faith, or fervency?

Yet we have kids to feed, bills to pay, deadlines to meet.

The calendar pounces on our good intentions like a tiger on a rabbit. We want to pray, but *when*?

We want to pray, but *why*? We might as well admit it. Prayer is odd, peculiar. Speaking into space. Lifting words into the sky. We can't even get the cable company to answer us, yet God will? The doctor is too busy, but God isn't? We have our doubts about prayer.

And we have our checkered history with prayer: unmet expectations, unanswered requests. We can barely genuflect for the scar tissue on our knees. God, to some, is the ultimate heartbreaker. Why keep tossing the coins of our longings into a silent pool? He jilted me once . . . but not twice.

Oh, the peculiar puzzle of prayer.

We aren't the first to struggle. The sign-up sheet for Prayer 101 contains some familiar names: the apostles John, James, Andrew, and Peter. When one of Jesus' disciples requested, "Lord, teach us to pray" (Luke 11:1 NIV), none of the others objected. No one walked away saying, "Hey, I have prayer figured out." The first followers of Jesus needed prayer guidance.

The first followers of Jesus needed prayer guidance.

In fact, the only tutorial they ever requested was on prayer. They could have asked for instructions on many topics: bread multiplying, speech making, storm stilling. Jesus raised people from the dead. But a "How to Vacate the Cemetery" seminar? His followers never called for one. But they did want him to do this: "Lord, teach us to pray."

Might their interest have had something to do with the jaw-dropping, eye-popping promises Jesus attached to prayer? "Ask and it will be given to you" (Matt. 7:7 NIV). "If you believe, you will get anything you ask for in prayer" (Matt. 21:22 NCV). Jesus never attached such power to other endeavors. "*Plan* and it will be given to you." "You will get anything you *work* for." Those words are not in the Bible. But these are—"If you remain in me and follow my teachings, you can ask anything you want, and it will be given to you" (John 15:7 NCV).

Jesus gave stunning prayer promises.

And he set a compelling prayer example. Jesus prayed before he ate. He prayed for children. He prayed for the sick. He prayed with thanks. He prayed with tears. He had made the planets and shaped the stars, yet he prayed. He is the Lord of angels and Commander of heavenly hosts, yet he prayed. He is coequal with God, the exact representation of the Holy One, and yet he devoted himself to prayer. He prayed in the desert, cemetery, and garden. "He went out and departed to a solitary place; and there He prayed" (Mark 1:35).

This dialogue must have been common among his friends:

"Has anyone seen Jesus?"

"Oh, you know. He's up to the same thing."

"Praying *again*?"

"Yep. He's been gone since sunrise."

Jesus would even disappear for an entire night of prayer. I'm thinking of one occasion in particular. He'd just experienced one of the most stressful days of his ministry. The day began with the news of the death of his relative John the Baptist. Jesus sought to retreat with his disciples, yet a throng of thousands followed him. Though grief-stricken, he spent the day teaching and healing people. When it was discovered that the host of people had no food to eat, Jesus multiplied bread out of a basket and fed the entire multitude. In the span of a few hours, he battled sorrow, stress, demands, and needs. He deserved a good night's rest. Yet when evening finally came, he told the crowd to leave and the disciples to board their boat, and "he went up into the hills by himself to pray" (Mark 6:46 NLT).

Apparently it was the correct choice. A storm exploded over the Sea of Galilee, leaving the disciples "in trouble far away from land, for a strong wind had risen, and they were fighting heavy waves. About three o'clock in the morning Jesus came toward them, walking on the water" (Matt. 14:24–25 NLT). Jesus ascended the mountain depleted. He reappeared invigorated. When he reached the water, he never broke his stride. You'd have thought the water was a park lawn and the storm a spring breeze.

Do you think the disciples made the prayer–power connection? "Lord, teach us to pray *like that*. Teach us to find strength in prayer. To banish fear in prayer. To defy storms in prayer. To come off the mountain of prayer with the authority of a prince."

What about you? The disciples faced angry waves and a watery grave. You face angry clients, a turbulent economy, raging seas of stress and sorrow.

"Lord," we still request, "teach us to pray."

When the disciples asked Jesus to teach them to pray, he gave them a prayer. Not a lecture on prayer. Not the doctrine of prayer. He gave them a quotable, repeatable, portable prayer (Luke 11:1–4).

Could you use the same? It seems to me that the prayers of the Bible can be distilled into one. The result is a simple, easy-to-remember, pocket-size prayer:

Father,

> *you are good.*
>> *I need help. Heal me and forgive me.*
>>> *They need help.*
>>>> *Thank you.*
>>>>> *In Jesus' name, amen.*

Let this prayer punctuate your day. As you begin your morning, *Father, you are good.* As you commute to work or walk the hallways at school, *I need help.* As you wait in the grocery line, *They need help.* Keep this prayer in your pocket as you pass through the day.

When we invite God into our world, he walks in. He brings

a host of gifts: joy, patience, resilience. Anxieties come, but they don't stick. Fears surface and then depart. Regrets land on the windshield, but then comes the wiper of prayer. The devil still hands me stones of guilt, but I turn and give them to Christ. I'm completing my sixth decade, yet I'm wired with energy. I am happier, healthier, and more hopeful than I have ever been. Struggles come, for sure. But so does God.

Prayer is not a privilege for the pious, not the art of a chosen few. Prayer is simply a heartfelt conversation between God and his child.

Prayer is not a privilege for the pious, not the art of a chosen few. Prayer is simply a heartfelt conversation between God and his child. My friend, he wants to talk with you. Even now, as you read these words, he taps at the door. Open it. Welcome him in. Let the conversation begin.

Prayers for Home
and Family

1

May the LORD watch between you and me
when we are absent one from another.

GENESIS 31:49

Father in heaven, your ways are not our ways, and your thoughts are so much higher than ours. Your wisdom is beyond anyone's understanding.

The military life is not easy. The time away from my family and my home is so hard, Lord. Please help me stay connected with my family so that our bonds remain strong. Keep my loved ones and my relationship with you at the forefront of my thoughts when I am away. Enable me to serve and to do my job, knowing that you are watching over those at home.

Please be with my family when I'm deployed or when I have to leave them. Remove the worry and fear, and replace it with your peace and comfort. Assure them that you are in control. Bless them today, Lord.

Thank you, Jesus, for watching over us.

In your name I pray, amen.

2

---

*Love suffers long and is kind; love does not envy;
love does not parade itself, is not puffed up; does
not behave rudely, does not seek its own, is not
provoked, thinks no evil; does not rejoice in iniquity,
but rejoices in the truth; bears all things, believes
all things, hopes all things, endures all things.*

1 Corinthians 13:4-7

Lord, you are the perfect expression of love. Your love never ends, and your love never fails. Your love conquers all.

Help me understand what real love means and how to express that love to you and to the people in my life. Give me wisdom to know when to turn off the intense warrior side that I need for my job and simply love the way you love. Help me serve, never forgetting to love as you teach us in your Word.

My desire is that our family will be filled with an abundance of love—true, godly love—for one another and for you. Please bless those at home that they, too, will seek to love as you do.

Thank you for loving us first and bringing us into your family. Thank you for teaching us through your Son what love really is.

In Christ's name, amen.

3

Do not worry, saying, "What shall we eat?" or "What shall we drink?" or "What shall we wear?" For after all these things the Gentiles seek. For your heavenly Father knows that you need all these things.

MATTHEW 6:31-32

My father in heaven, you are the ultimate provider. You see the needs of your people and bless them mightily out of the abundance of your love.

I confess, Lord, that I worry too often about how I will pay my bills, put food on the table, and prepare for the future. Help me trust in you as my provider and not stress out about the things of this world. Teach me to rely on you and your guidance for our provision and to appreciate the job you have given me so I can earn a living.

Remind my family that you are their ultimate provider. As you meet their needs, may they give you the glory and honor for providing for them.

Thank you for taking such great care of us.

In your Son's name I pray, amen.

4

If you bring your gift to the altar, and there remember that your brother has something against you, leave your gift there before the altar, and go your way. First be reconciled to your brother, and then come and offer your gift.

MATTHEW 5:23-24

L ord God, you are the holy Redeemer. You have given us the perfect example of forgiveness and reconciliation in your Son, Jesus.

I have held on to many grudges and old grievances and hurts, Lord. I fear that they get in the way of my walk with you, but I struggle to forgive as you would have me do. I need your help. Please show me how to forgive and heal. Help me let go of the toxic attitudes that heavy my heart and threaten my peace.

In my family, like most, we've had conflicts and unresolved issues. Help us today to put aside past hurts and to reconcile. Heal us, Lord, and restore our relationships.

Thank you for showing us what forgiveness and reconciliation really look like. Thank you for healing our old wounds and helping us move forward.

In Jesus' name, amen.

5

Choose for yourselves this day whom you will serve, whether the gods which your fathers served that were on the other side of the River, or the gods of the Amorites, in whose land you dwell. But as for me and my house, we will serve the LORD.

JOSHUA 24:15

Almighty God, you are worthy of all worship and honor. You are the only true God, the King of the universe.

Lord, help me follow you with my whole heart. Give me the passion and courage to choose to serve you all my days. May I have the boldness to stand strong regardless of what others think. May I not be swayed by people's opinions or the way the wind is blowing in our culture and the world around us. Help me stand firm with you.

Strengthen my loved ones at home to serve you only, Lord. Guide my family to be committed to you so that we stand together, proclaiming your Word.

Thank you for strengthening our faith and our resolve to follow you. Thank you for your faithfulness.

In Jesus' name I pray, amen.

6

Bear one another's burdens, and
so fulfill the law of Christ.

GALATIANS 6:2

Heavenly Father, your yoke is easy, and your burden is light. You carry your people in times of trouble and pain.

Lord, I often forget to pray for my family and friends as I should. Whether I'm deployed or at home or in the field, I'm grateful I can always pray for them. I can still be supportive of those who need me, those you have placed in my life. Give me the heart to see others I can help, and take my focus off me and my problems. Help me be a prayer warrior for those who need me.

You know the concerns and burdens my family and friends are struggling with right now. Please intercede for them, and let them feel your presence.

Thank you for hearing our prayers and placing us together to share one another's burdens.

In Christ's holy name, amen.

7

---

*I have come that they may have life, and
that they may have it more abundantly.*

JOHN 10:10

Our father, you are the God who pours out his love and mercies on his people. You guide them with your gentle, loving hand.

I want to live a full life with all the blessings, joy, and purpose you have for me, Lord. At the end of my life, I want to know that I have lived it well and have honored you, served my country, and been a blessing to my family. Help me know your abundant life. Lead me to the scriptures that can guide me in the right direction so my life will always stay on the course you have set for me.

Direct the steps of my family today. Help them to see your amazing blessings in their lives and to have the abundant life in you.

Thank you for filling our days with purpose and blessings and joy.

In Jesus' name, amen.

Prayers for Duty
and Courage

8

Greater love has no one than this, than
to lay down one's life for his friends.

John 15:13

God, you are the supreme warrior. Your mighty hands will bring true justice and peace to the world in your good time.

Lord, I believe you have called me to serve my country and place my life on the line if necessary. Please strengthen my spirit, my mind, and my body so I can serve with honor and distinction. I pray I never have to enter the field of battle, but if I do, remind me that I am secure in you no matter what. Enable me to put the needs of my friends and the people in my unit ahead of my own. Let them see you in my service.

Please give peace and comfort to my loved ones and friends. Remind them that our lives are in your loving hands.

Thank you for strengthening me and showing me true love through your Son's sacrifice.

In Jesus' name, amen.

9

---

*Have I not commanded you? Be strong
and of good courage; do not be afraid,
nor be dismayed, for the LORD your
God is with you wherever you go.*

JOSHUA 1:9

Lord, your strength and authority are without limits. You cast out all fear, and you fill your people with boldness and power.

Help me, Lord, not to be gripped and controlled by fear. When frightening times come, please remind me that you are with me. Set my eyes and my heart on your promise that you will never leave me or forsake me. Help me trust you with my very life so I can serve without fear or hesitation. Go before me like a light, and shine in the very dark places I am called to enter.

Please be with my family and chase their fears away. Comfort them and give them peace when I'm absent.

Thank you for being with me today and every day. I am grateful for your promises and your guidance.

In your Son's holy name, amen.

10

The LORD is my strength and my shield;
my heart trusted in Him, and I am helped;
therefore my heart greatly rejoices, and
with my song I will praise Him.

PSALM 28:7

Father, you never leave us. You never forsake us. You are the God who protects his people. You are worthy of all praise and honor.

I confess that I rely too often on my own strength and training. I don't trust you first and foremost. Help me place my entire faith and hope in you as my shield and my strength. Teach me to pray and follow your Spirit and rely on you.

Keep watch over my loved ones at home. When things seem dark and overwhelming, pull them closer to you under your shelter of protection, comfort, and love. Teach them to lean on you during those times.

Thank you for going ahead of me into the darkness. Thank you for covering me and my family with your power and your truth.

In Christ's name, amen.

11

He teaches my hands to make war, so that
my arms can bend a bow of bronze.

PSALM 18:34

Heavenly Father, you know the hearts and intentions of all people, and your justice is perfect and righteous. Your plans will reign supreme.

I yearn for peace but prepare for war. Sharpen my skills and strengthen my hands and my heart for my job so I can defend my country and its people. Guide my spirit to be one of service to you and my nation.

My family needs you. I have to train so often, and my job requires a lot of time away. Help them understand and be able to manage the days I am away. Reassure them that I'm following your will for my life.

Thank you for the privilege of being in the military. I am so grateful for what this job has done for me and how it has shaped me.

In your name, amen.

12

Though one may be overpowered by another, two can withstand him. And a threefold cord is not quickly broken.

ECCLESIASTES 4:12

Gracious Father, you are the Great Deliverer and my true salvation. You parted a sea and walked your people through it. Nothing is beyond your mighty reach.

Help me serve not only you and my nation but those in my unit as well. Bind us together so we can work as one. Make us strong and resolute in our duty to stand between evil and our friends, families, and countrymen. Teach us to stand firm in the face of all challenges.

Please protect my friends and those in all the branches of the service. Let them know you are always with them. Reassure them that their service is good and noble. Bless their families and give them peace and comfort.

Thank you for the incredible men and women with whom you have allowed me to serve. May I always be faithful to you and to them.

In your holy name, amen.

13

---

*Yea, though I walk through the valley
of the shadow of death, I will fear no
evil; for You are with me; Your rod
and Your staff, they comfort me.*

PSALM 23:4

God, you have given us the Comforter. You ease the concerns of your people. Death has no power, because you hold the keys to death and hades.

Lord, sometimes I am called to serve in evil places and very tense and challenging situations. Please walk with me in those times, and keep me calm and focused so I won't fear the evil I must face.

I can imagine what my family must feel while I'm serving. Don't let the fear of the unknown and other unrelenting concerns overcome them. Grant them reassurance and serenity.

I am thankful for the confidence that comes from knowing you. Thank you for being with me as I do my best to serve my country and honor my commitment to you.

In Jesus' name, amen.

14

I heard the voice of the Lord, saying: "Whom shall I send, and who will go for Us?" Then I said, "Here am I! Send me."

ISAIAH 6:8

Holy, holy, holy are you, Lord Almighty. You are high above all people. Let them praise your name forever.

I am here, Lord. Send me—not just in my job but in my life. I haven't always made myself fully available to you and your will. Please forgive me and change my heart so I will go where you would have me go and stay where you would have me stay. I do not want to hold back from you in any part of my life.

May the little ones at home be filled with the desire to serve you. Let the spirit of our home be one of boldness and courage and faith. Continue to minister to them.

Thank you for guiding my steps and placing me where you have. I am grateful for the opportunities to serve you today and tomorrow and beyond.

In your mighty name, amen.

Prayers for Protection and Guidance

15

---

*Put on the whole armor of God, that you may be
able to stand against the wiles of the devil. For
we do not wrestle against flesh and blood, but
against principalities, against powers, against the
rulers of the darkness of this age, against spiritual
hosts of wickedness in the heavenly places.*

EPHESIANS 6:11-12

Heavenly Father, your power knows no limits. Your enemies tremble at the mere thought of you. You are my God and my Savior, and my hope is in you all day long.

I need every piece of your armor to protect me, Lord. I know the evil I fight starts in the spiritual kingdom. Though I am trained for war, I am way out of my league. Please give me your spiritual protection. Prepare me to face all my challenges, both physical and spiritual.

My family has a hard time understanding the enemy I prepare to face. Please protect them and give them peace. Lead them to the Scriptures to calm their worries and concerns.

Thank you for protecting my family and me. I am so grateful you have prepared me for whatever is to come.

In your name, amen.

16

He shall give His angels charge over you, to keep you in all your ways. In their hands they shall bear you up, lest you dash your foot against a stone.

PSALM 91:11-12

Father, you are the defender of your people and the upholder of righteousness. I am powerless without you.

I am called to dangerous places where I need your supernatural protection. Please put angels around me to guard me from the seen and unseen dangers in my life. Let them shield and guide me and those in my unit. Keep us safe as we do our jobs.

Surround my family with your angelic warriors. Keep the evil one far from them, and give my loved ones comfort in knowing that you fight for them. Protect every step they take today.

Thank you for using your army of angels to care for us and fight for us. I am grateful for the many ways you watch over my family and me.

In Christ's holy name, amen.

17

God is our refuge and strength, a
very present help in trouble.

PSALM 46:1

G od, you are the origin of all that is good, righteous, and true. You are high above all nations and all peoples. You are a sanctuary for those who call on your name.

I confess that there are days I feel my spirit and resolve weaken. I have so much pressure from my job and the expectations of serving my country. I desperately need your strength to uphold me and renew my spirit. Please remind me to be anxious for nothing because you are near. Lead me through this tough period.

Protect my family today. Shield them from trouble and the worries of the world. Teach them to rest in your promises so they will have peace.

I am extremely grateful for your gentle spirit, which can calm the raging seas around us. Thank you for your unfailing love and support.

In Jesus' name, amen.

18

"Because he loves me," says the LORD,
"I will rescue him; I will protect him,
for he acknowledges my name."

PSALM 91:14 NIV

Heavenly Father, you are compassionate and patient with your people. You redeem and guard your own. Your mercies are new every day.

As I serve, please protect me in all aspects of my life—my job, my family, my spiritual walk, and my very life. Direct my prayer life, and continue to teach me to follow you better. Help me acknowledge you in everything I do, and let me rest in your divine protection.

Strengthen those at home. Their concerns are different than mine but just as important and worrisome for them. Teach them to continually praise you and your name regardless of what they face. May they walk through their day with a bold confidence that you are watching over them.

Thank you for revealing yourself to us. I am so grateful that you chose to save me and that you continually look after me.

In your Son's name, amen.

19

I will call upon the L<small>ORD</small>, who is worthy to be praised; so shall I be saved from my enemies.

2 S<small>AMUEL</small> 22:4

My father, you know every breath I will take and the length of my days. You order my every step. You alone are my God and my Savior.

Help me resist the temptations of the evil one. I can face the enemies in the field, but the unseen Enemy is warring for my soul. Don't let me follow his plans, and protect me from my own foolish and, at times, wayward heart as well. Teach me to rely on you to keep my greatest adversary at bay.

Place a special protection around those who serve with me and in all the other branches. Let them see your divine shield all around them. Be their guide and their guardian.

I am so grateful that you watch over me and keep me focused on you. Thank you for giving us wisdom on how to face our challenges.

In your holy name, amen.

20

You must not fear them, for the LORD
your God Himself fights for you.

DEUTERONOMY 3:22

Father, I lift up your name and give you praise! You are the King whose greatness is unsearchable. You defend those you love.

I know you are in front of me in the battle. Give me the courage to face any trials and obstacles the Enemy throws my way. Quell my fears and concerns. Encourage me to remain strong in you and your plan for my life. Help me be fearless in the face of the Adversary and his schemes.

Fight on behalf of my family. Wage war on whatever seeks to cause them harm or to place a wedge between you and them. Keep them safe and close to you.

Thank you for leading the way in my life and my career. I rejoice in knowing that you hate evil and will someday bring it to an end.

In Jesus' name, amen.

21

---

*He went a little farther, and fell on the
ground, and prayed that if it were possible,
the hour might pass from Him. And He said,
"Abba, Father, all things are possible for You.
Take this cup away from Me; nevertheless,
not what I will, but what You will."*

MARK 14:35-36

G od, you love us so much that you did not spare even your own Son. The depth and scope of your love are unimaginable to my mind.

Jesus, help me strive to be obedient and to trust God just as you did when you set the supreme example. Work in my spirit so I will desire to follow the will of God wherever it leads, no matter how hard it might be. Teach me the humility and love I need to serve my God like this. I want my will to conform to your will.

Fill the ones back home with your love and mercy today. Renew their hearts with a deep appreciation for what you have done for them and for all of us.

Thank you for demonstrating true submission and reverence. I am grateful for the amazing work you did on the cross and are doing in my life.

In your holy name, amen.

Prayers for Perseverance and Faith

22

---

*Count it all joy when you fall into various
trials, knowing that the testing of your
faith produces patience. But let patience
have its perfect work, that you may be
perfect and complete, lacking nothing.*

JAMES 1:2-4

God, your love can never be matched. Your every thought and desire are for our good. Each of your works is a blessing and a masterpiece.

Every day there seem to be new challenges to my faith. I often wonder if I can stand up to them, and sometimes I don't. Help the trials in my life to do their perfect work in me. Change my attitude toward difficulties and testing so I see they are there not to break me but to make me stronger, to build me up.

Fill those at home with joy today as they work through their hardships. May they have fresh outlooks and transformed spirits.

Thank you for being our rock during the storms of life. Thank you for the promises you have made to us in your Word.

In your Son's holy name, amen.

23

You therefore must endure hardship
as a good soldier of Jesus Christ.

2 TIMOTHY 2:3

Heavenly Father, you have legions of angels at your command, and all the forces of nature serve you. Yet you still listen to and love your people.

The calling you have given me is not without serious challenges. Strengthen me to face each obstacle in a way that will honor you. Help me not only to serve my country through difficult circumstances but also to serve you through the tough times. Increase my trust in your Word and assurances.

Be with my family at home today. Anything that impacts me, impacts them. Remind them that you are in control at all times. Remove any fears or doubts and replace them with patience and faith.

Thank you for placing me in my circumstances. I am grateful you have prepared me to face anything that comes my way.

In Jesus' name, amen.

24

I am persuaded that neither death nor life,
nor angels nor principalities nor powers,
nor things present nor things to come, nor
height nor depth, nor any other created thing,
shall be able to separate us from the love
of God which is in Christ Jesus our Lord.

ROMANS 8:38-39

Lord, every believer rests securely in your love. No one can snatch a single soul from your powerful hand.

Remind me that nothing stands between us. Because of my sins and the world around me, I get discouraged and sometimes believe I have done too much for you to love me. Help me keep that lie out of my thoughts, and let the depth of your love sink into my mind and my heart so I will never doubt again.

Shower your peace and love on those at home. Show them that your love covers them in every circumstance. Wrap your arms around them, and give them the confidence that they are always yours.

I am grateful you love us so much that nothing will ever come between us. Thank you for fighting for me and never giving up on me.

In Christ's name, amen.

25

Therefore confess your sins to each other and pray for each other so that you may be healed. The prayer of a righteous person is powerful and effective.

JAMES 5:16 NIV

Father, you lead your people and hear their prayers. You know each of your sheep by name. You are the great and wonderful Shepherd.

Help me find a trustworthy prayer partner. I too often try to go it alone, and I'm reluctant to share my spiritual life with others. Please change my heart. Give me a passion to reach out to other Christians so we can pray for each other and seek your will together.

Help those in my unit. Ignite a desire in them to know you. Use me there, and raise up Christians in our midst. I pray that those who serve around me will come to know you.

Thank you for putting people in our paths who can walk this road of faith with us. Thank you for all the believers worldwide. May your mighty name continue to spread throughout the earth.

In Jesus' holy name, amen.

26

I know the thoughts that I think toward you, says the LORD, thoughts of peace and not of evil, to give you a future and a hope.

JEREMIAH 29:11

Dear Father, from the beginning of time, you have planned the path your people would take. Your infinite mind thought of me long before I was born. I am humbled by your incredible love.

I struggle with doubts and fear about my future. I don't trust you nearly as much as I should. Please forgive me and reinforce my faith in you. Help me understand and believe that you are in control and have a good plan for me, my family, and my career.

Bless my family today. Help them know that all things rest in your hands and that you always have their best interests in mind. Don't let them fear the future.

Thank you for ordering our steps and guiding our way. I am thankful to know that your thoughts are always for our good.

In your Son's name, amen.

27

For we walk by faith, not by sight.

2 CORINTHIANS 5:7

Jesus, how magnificent your name is in all the earth. A time will come when every knee will bow and every tongue will confess that you are Lord.

Help me walk in true faith. Too often I guide my life by my own pride and selfish desires. Teach me to trust you fully and to live according to your will. Give me the discipline and desire to search the Scriptures and to pray daily to know you better.

Draw my family closer to you today. Reveal yourself to them, and help them grow in their faith. May they seek an authentic and active relationship with you.

Thank you for drawing us ever closer to you and being the light for our path. I am so very thankful to be your child.

In your name I pray, amen.

28

---

*Peace I leave with you, My peace I give to you;
not as the world gives do I give to you. Let not
your heart be troubled, neither let it be afraid.*

John 14:27

Father, you are slow to anger, gracious in mercy, and abounding in love. You are worthy of all praise and honor.

I humbly ask for your peace in my life. Being in the service causes many sleepless nights and worries and concerns. I am in situations I can't control, and I regularly stand at evil's doorstep. Fill me with your peace, and reassure me that you are there and in control.

Comfort and bless my loved ones at home. They, too, have to endure the challenges of military life. Calm their spirits, and focus their hearts on you.

Thank you for caring about every part of our lives and every member of our families. Thank you for the Holy Spirit, who is our great comforter.

In Jesus' name, amen.

Prayers for Integrity and Honor

29

The righteous lead blameless lives;
blessed are their children after them.

PROVERBS 20:7 NIV

Heavenly Father, you love righteousness and justice. You have set before us what is right, true, and good. I praise your holy name!

Help me live a life of integrity and honor. I feel as though I fail so often. Forgive me, and strengthen my desire to follow your Word. Restore my spirit so I will always seek to do your will. I want to be an example to my family and those around me so that, through your work in me, they will want to follow you too.

Pour your Spirit on my family and friends today. Guide them to your truth, and help them come to know you better. Reassure them that you will never leave their side.

Thank you for giving us the Scriptures so we can know more about you, your law, and your character. I am grateful you have made your will known.

In Jesus' name, amen.

30

Let your conduct be without covetousness;
be content with such things as you have.

HEBREWS 13:5

God, every good and perfect gift is from you. You know exactly what your people desire and need. You are the Great Provider.

I really struggle with wanting more than I have. Forgive me, and show me how to be content with the blessings you have given me so I don't complain about what I don't have. Teach me to appreciate all you have done for me.

My family struggles with this too. The constant desire to have more and more can overwhelm all of us at times. Please reveal yourself to them, and help them find their fulfillment in you.

Thank you for always taking care of me. I am grateful for my health, my job, my family, and all the other good things you allow in my life.

In your Son's name, amen.

31

Whatever you do, do it heartily, as to the Lord and not to men, knowing that from the Lord you will receive the reward of the inheritance; for you serve the Lord Christ.

COLOSSIANS 3:23-24

Father, you are compassionate and gracious, slow to anger, and abounding in love. You have removed our sins as far as the east is from the west. How great is your unfailing love!

Some days are difficult, and I can become discouraged about my job. When that happens, help me regain my priorities and focus. Remind me why I serve my country and whom I am really doing this for. Change my attitude toward the work you have called me to do. Help me be passionate and professional in my service because I ultimately do it for you and those at home.

As I serve far away, continue to be with my family. Calm their spirits, and bless them as they, too, work for you. Increase their joy today.

Thank you for allowing me to work for my country and you. Thank you for showing me how important it is to serve with honor and distinction.

In your holy name, amen.

32

Above all else, guard your heart, for
everything you do flows from it.

PROVERBS 4:23 NIV

Lord, you have established your throne in heaven, and your kingdom is all the earth. I worship your holy name.

Forgive me for looking at images with lust and filling my mind and heart with things I shouldn't. Give me strength to resist the lure of sin that can be ever present on the computer, television, and so many other places. Guard my heart, and repair my spirit so I may live a godly life in all areas.

Protect the hearts of my family too. Keep the children pure, and don't let the evil one get a foothold in their lives. Give them wisdom and sound judgment so they will live honorably.

Thank you for being a forgiving God. I am so grateful to know that when I stumble and fall, you will pick me up and clean me off. Thank you for never giving up on me.

In Christ's name, amen.

33

Honor all people. Love the brotherhood.
Fear God. Honor the king.

1 Peter 2:17

Gracious Father, you are the King of kings and Lord of lords. Your majesty covers all the earth. I will serve you all my days.

Lord, please give me the humility and grace to serve those in authority over me—both you and my commanders. Remove any pride or conceit that would get in the way of my doing my duty and keeping my promises. Use my service to continually guide others to you.

Help the people in my unit stay positive and respectful toward authority. Sometimes we criticize and disrespect our leaders behind their backs. Guide our conversations and attitudes so that we give the respect due to those in charge. Let humility grow in our company.

I am especially thankful for the men and women who are great examples to me of godly service. Thank you for your continued guidance.

In Jesus' name, amen.

34

———

*Do not be conformed to this world, but be
transformed by the renewing of your mind.*

ROMANS 12:2

Father, you sit on your high throne surrounded by the angels, and yet you still teach us what is good and pleasing to you. Your gentle love can never be matched.

I feel bombarded by the world sometimes. Keep your Word and teachings fresh in my mind so I will not be deceived by the evil one. Help me stay focused on reading the Bible, and let it sink into my soul. I need to have your desires in the forefront of my mind.

Teach your Word and desires to those at home. Let studying Scripture be a priority for them, and give them the wisdom and understanding to make it real in their lives.

Thank you for showing us what is good and true. I am so grateful you have given us instructions on what is best for us.

In Jesus' name, amen.

Prayers for Wisdom
and Leadership

35

---

*If any of you lacks wisdom, you should ask
God, who gives generously to all without
finding fault, and it will be given to you.*

JAMES 1:5 NIV

Heavenly Father, you are the fountain of all that is good, right, and true. Your knowledge is limitless, and your understanding is without equal.

I humbly ask for wisdom, Lord. I need help living according to your instructions. Direct my understanding and knowledge. Show me what is right in your eyes, and give me the desire to stay on the path you have for me. Help me discipline myself to study your Word regularly.

Let my family's goal be to know your thoughts and plans for their lives. Place your Word in their hearts, and make it the foundation for their lives. Give them the joy of knowing you better.

I am extremely grateful that you have given us your instruction manual. Thank you for allowing us insight into your character, plan, and wisdom.

In Jesus' name, amen.

36

The way of a fool is right in his own eyes,
but he who heeds counsel is wise.

PROVERBS 12:15

Lord, you raise up nations, and you bring them low. You make kings, and you remove them from their thrones. The entire world is subject to your good and merciful will.

Help me find good mentors and friends, who will speak wisdom into my life. Reveal to me a good adviser at work so I can serve my command well and excel in my job. Let me always be a seeker of your perfect ways.

Guide my family to choose wisely those they seek counsel from and those they associate with. As they surround themselves with godly people and leaders, strengthen their fellowship and friendship.

Thank you for Christian community. I am grateful for the many people you have placed in my life who have had a great influence on me.

In Christ's name, amen.

37

---

*Whoever desires to become great among
you, let him be your servant.*

MATTHEW 20:26

G od, you command the power of life and death. You hold the stars and planets in place. Your power and majesty astound me.

I want to know how to be a good leader and role model. Please help me understand how to be a good servant leader. Keep me humble and my motives pure. Give me the wisdom and the heart to care for the people I lead. Develop my spirit so I will earn the respect of those I command.

Bless those in my unit. Be with my friends, and show yourself to them. Guide our missions and work so they can serve your will. Protect them from harm, and place angels around them.

I am thankful that you have given us godly examples of leadership. Thank you for instilling in me the yearning to lead and serve.

In Jesus' name, amen.

38

You shall select from all the people able men, such as fear God, men of truth, hating covetousness; and place such over them to be rulers of thousands, rulers of hundreds, rulers of fifties, and rulers of tens.

EXODUS 18:21

Heavenly Father, I am so in awe of you and how you take care of all of us. Every day I discover something new to worship about you.

Create in me the character I need to be a leader. I often feel that I am not worthy of my job and my responsibilities. Please grow my character so I am able to lead those around me and earn their respect. Teach me through your Word the lessons I need.

Let the principles of this scripture take hold in our command. Encourage our commanders to pursue your character and will. Watch over our leaders that they will not be swayed by their personal desires. Teach them your ways.

Thank you for appointing those in charge and preparing their hearts for leadership.

In Jesus' name, amen.

39

Let your "Yes" be "Yes," and your "No," "No."

MATTHEW 5:37

Father, you are without error or blemish. You are perfect in all your ways, and the works of your hands are flawless. The heavens declare your glory.

Help me be a person of conviction and truth. Teach me to always keep my word so I can be trusted in everything I say and do. Let those who serve under me know I will always seek to follow your Word when I am in charge. Reveal to me any character issues or weaknesses I need to address.

Protect my fellow servicemen and servicewomen around the world as they deal with many conflicts right now. Watch over them, and if they don't know you, use this time to bring them into a saving knowledge of your Son.

Thank you for showing us the way of godly leadership. Thank you for encouraging me to excel.

In Jesus' name, amen.

40

I am the vine; you are the branches. If you remain in me and I in you, you will bear much fruit; apart from me you can do nothing.

JOHN 15:5 NIV

Father, you pursue your children when they stray, and you run and embrace them when they return. Your grace and mercy are unending.

I too often allow myself to become separated from you, and I try to live my way. Forgive me and keep my feet on the right path. Don't let any obstacles get in the way of my relationship with you. Help me to bear good fruit and to be useful to you. Keep me connected to you always.

I pray that the ones at home will remain committed to you. Keep them close, and continue to pour your love and mercies on them. Bless my friends and fellow servicemen and servicewomen. May your hand always protect them.

Thank you for keeping us close to you and helping us grow. I am grateful for your loving grace in my life.

In your holy name, amen.

About Max Lucado

More than 120 million readers have found inspiration and encouragement in the writings of Max Lucado. He lives with his wife, Denalyn, and their mischievous mutt, Andy, in San Antonio, Texas, where he serves the people of Oak Hills Church. Visit his website at MaxLucado.com or follow him at Twitter.com/MaxLucado and Facebook.com/MaxLucado.

About Mark Mynheir

Mark Mynheir is a former Marine and a career police officer, who has served as a narcotics agent, a S.W.A.T. Team member, and a homicide detective. Mark also divides his time as an author, having published five novels and multiple magazine articles (www.copwriter.com). He has been married for more than twenty-five years to the love of his life, Lori, and they have three fantastic children—Chris, Shannon, and Justin.

Discover Even More Power
in a Simple Prayer

ISBN 978-0-7180-7812-6

$15.99

Join Max Lucado on a journey to the very heart of biblical prayer and discover rest in the midst of chaos and confidence even for prayer wimps.

Available wherever books are sold.

BeforeAmen.com

Make Your Prayers Personal

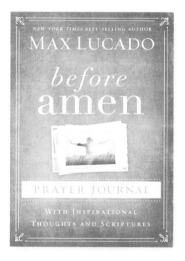

ISBN 978-0-7180-1406-3

$13.99

This beautiful companion journal to *Before Amen* helps readers stoke their prayer life. It features quotes and scriptures to inspire both prayer warriors and those who struggle to pray.

Tools for Your Church and Small Group

Before Amen: A DVD Study

ISBN 978-0-529-12342-8

$21.99

Max Lucado leads this four-session study through his discovery of a simple tool for connecting with God each day. This study will help small-group participants build their prayer life, calm the chaos of their world, and grow in Christ.

Before Amen Study Guide

ISBN 978-0-529-12334-3

$9.99

This guide is filled with Scripture study, discussion questions, and practical ideas designed to help small-group members understand Jesus' teaching on prayer. An integral part of the *Before Amen* small-group study, it will help group members build prayer into their everyday lives.

Before Amen
Church Campaign Kit

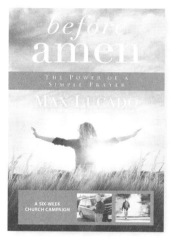

ISBN 978-0-529-12369-5

$49.99

The church campaign kit includes a four-session DVD study by Max Lucado; a study guide with discussion questions and video notes; the *Before Amen* trade book; a getting started guide; and access to a website with all the sermon resources churches need to launch and sustain a four-week *Before Amen* campaign.

Before Amen for Everyone

Before Amen Audiobook

ISBN 978-1-4915-4662-8 | $19.99

Enjoy the unabridged audio CD of *Before Amen*.

Before Amen eBook

ISBN 978-0-529-12390-9

Read *Before Amen* anywhere on your favorite tablet or electronic device.

Antes del amén Spanish Edition

ISBN 978-0-7180-0157-5 | $13.99

The hope of *Before Amen* is also available for Spanish-language readers.